EMILY DICKINSON VS. SARA TEASDALE

Eight Lines at a Time

EMILY DICKINSON VS. SARA TEASDALE

Eight Lines at a Time

A face-to-face selection of short poems by two
of the most iconic American female authors

Selected by
Valeska Matti

Dedicated to all female poets who got inspired by the verses of Emily and Sara.

TABLE OF CONTENTS

PREFACE

This is the second anthology of poetry that I have compiled. After my first one, "100 Poems every Child -and Adult- should Know", which is a rather broad selection in terms of authors, styles, themes, and levels of complexity, I wanted to do something more specific and special. While exploring the vast universe of Classic Poetry, several female authors have always caught my attention, particularly when comparing their different ways to portray their own universes in their writing.

That's when the thought came to mind, of putting together a vis-à-vis, a face-to-face showcase of the work of two of my favorite writers of those times: the renowned and acclaimed Emily Dickinson, and the somewhat less recognized, oftentimes neglected Sara Teasdale. I found so many pieces by both poets, which addressed the same matter so differently, that the idea of contrasting their poems, one to one, sounded like a challenge worth pursuing.

Both Emily and Sara were born into accommodated families, and both got involved with poetry from their early ages, but that's pretty much as far as their similarities go. Strictly speaking, they were not contemporaries, as Teasdale had not even turned two by the time Dickinson died. Dickinson didn't publish almost any of her work in her lifetime, however gained tremendous fame post-mortem. Teasdale, on the other hand, published several collections of poems, one of which was recognized with what would later be the Pulitzer Prize for Poetry. Her work, however, has been neglected by many scholars of more recent times.

Dickinson, unmarried and secluded, reached the end of her life with melancholy and depression, yet died from illness in her bed. Teasdale, who lived a somewhat more conventional life, and enjoyed success in her career as a writer, ended her own life.

Their different lives are also reflected in their different ways of writing poetry. Sara was known for her simplicity and classical forms. Emily had a style of her own, which defied conventions and disregarded literary rules.

Dickinson wrote about the seasons and the elements of nature in a very descriptive way. Teasdale very often utilized them as metaphors to talk about love and emotions.

In Sara's work you will read a lot about love: love that was, love that could be, love that wasn't. Emily wrote more regularly about disenchantment. She wrote plenty about God and faith, and about loss and death. For Sara, love can still be unconditional after death, and even death itself can have a positive tone, such as in *I will not Care* or *If Death is Kind*. I had to filter out many death-related pieces from Dickinson, to try and keep this face-to-face closer to a balance.

To ease the task of comparing the poems, if that is even possible, I have selected only 8-line pieces for the entire anthology. I have also attempted to match the poems' themes for every pair of facing pages of this book. Such matching is only possible to a certain extent, as the available volume of work for certain topics is not always comparable for both authors.

This is my humble tribute to the work of these two great representatives of -female- American literature. I invite you to enjoy it, while imagining how they both succeeded to reflect their own realities with such beauty and art... eight lines at a time.

I sincerely hope you will enjoy this selection.

Valeska Matti

EMILY ELIZABETH DICKINSON (1830 – 1886)

Emily Dickinson was born into the privileged life of a prominent family of Amherst, Massachusetts, on December 10, 1830. She was well educated for a woman of her time, attending high school and a year of college. Unlike most women of her social class, she didn't get married or have children, although she is believed to have had some love affairs. During the 1850s, Dickinson's most affectionate relationship was with her sister-in-law, Susan Gilbert. Many scholars interpret their relationship as a romantic one.

From an early age, Dickinson chose to restrict her social engagements and, as of her twenties, she chose to stay within her family home for most of the time. She had some friends but communicated with them mostly through letters. Eventually, she became a recluse, avoiding other people as much as possible. She took to wearing all-white clothing and rarely left her bedroom. That's where she composed most of her poetry.

Dickinson began writing in her early 20s but did not truly blossom as a poet until her 30s. In 1862 alone, she wrote 366 poems, approximately one per day.

Dickinson was also an avid naturalist in her own right. She was extremely fond of gardening. In fact, during her lifetime she was known for her skills in gardening and botany rather than for her poetry.

Over time, a sequence of losses and deaths in her closest circle of family and friends brought her spirits down. On May 15, 1886, after being confined to her bed for several months, Emily Dickinson died at the age of 55, from inflammatory kidney disease.

Only 10 of her 1800 poems were published before her death. Perhaps this lack of intention to publish is the reason many of her poems do not have a title (they were published using numbers or their first lines, as titles). Only after Emily died did her younger sister discover her collections of poetry and began the process of making them public. Since then, Emily Dickinson's fame has only grown, and she is now regarded as one of the most important figures in American poetry, one of the most widely read poets in the English language, and perhaps the most famous female poet.

Dickinson truly invented a unique writing style. She disregarded many common literary rules by experimenting with unconventional capitalization and punctuation. She used original wordplay, unexpected rhymes, and abrupt line breaks.

Dickinson's poetry frequently used humor, puns, irony, and satire, and because of the variety of her themes, her work does not fit conveniently into any one genre. That said, morbidity seems to be one of the most prevailing themes. Many of Dickinson's poems reflect her lifelong fascination with illness, dying, and death. Her poetry includes some of the English language's most vivid and sensitive descriptions of the human experience.

- Emily Elizabeth Dickinson -

SARA TREVOR TEASDALE (1884 – 1933)

Sara Teasdale was born on August 8, 1884, in St. Louis, Missouri, to a wealthy and devout family. She grew up in a determinedly religious household and was educated privately.

Teasdale was involved with literature and poetry since she was a young woman. Her first poem was published in a local newspaper in 1907. Her first collection of poems, "Sonnets to Duse and Other Poems", was published that same year. Teasdale's second collection, "Helen of Troy and Other Poems", was published in 1911, and it was well received by critics, who praised its lyrical mastery and romantic subject matter.

In 1914, Teasdale married Ernst Filsinger, a longtime admirer of her poetry, and moved with him to New York in 1916.

In 1918 she won the first Columbia Poetry Prize for her poetry collection "Love Songs", receiving public admiration for her well-crafted lyrical poetry, which centered on a woman's changing perspectives on beauty, love, and death. This prize would later be renamed as the Pulitzer Prize for Poetry; therefore Teasdale is considered to have been the first-ever winner thereof.

Filsinger's constant business travel caused Teasdale much loneliness. In 1929 she moved interstate for three months, to satisfy the criterion to gain a divorce. After that, she lived the rest of her life semi-invalid. In 1933, she took her own life, overdosing on sleeping pills.

Teasdale wrote a total of seven books of poetry. Although during her lifetime she was popular with both the public and critics, some later scholars found Teasdale's poetry unsophisticated, some of them even labeling her more as a singer than as a poet.

Many of Teasdale's poems portray developments in her own life, from her experiences as a young woman in St. Louis, to those as a successful yet increasingly uneasy writer in New York, to a depressed and disillusioned person who would, as said, end up committing suicide.

Teasdale's work has been characterized by its simplicity and clarity, her use of classical forms, musical language, and evocative emotion, as well as her passionate and romantic subject matter.

Teasdale's poems are consistently classical in style. She wrote technically excellent, pure, openhearted lyrics, usually in such conventional verse forms as quatrains or sonnets.

- Sara Trevor Teasdale -

I

OF LOVE, HEARTBRAKE, AND FAITH

*"It is strange how often a heart must be broken
before the years can make it wise."*

Sara Teasdale

1. JOY

I am wild, I will sing to the trees,
I will sing to the stars in the sky,
I love, I am loved, he is mine,
Now at last I can die!

I am sandaled with wind and with flame,
I have heart-fire and singing to give,
I can tread on the grass or the stars,
Now at last I can live!

SARA TEASDALE

2. DESIRE

Who never wanted, -- maddest joy
Remains to him unknown:
The banquet of abstemiousness
Surpasses that of wine.

Within its hope, though yet ungrasped
Desire's perfect goal,
No nearer, lest reality
Should disenthrall thy soul.

EMILY DICKINSON

3. GIFTS

I gave my first love laughter,
I gave my second tears,
I gave my third love silence
Through all the years.

My first love gave me singing,
My second eyes to see,
But oh, it was my third love
Who gave my soul to me.

SARA TEASDALE

4. MINE

Mine by the right of the white election!
Mine by the royal seal!
Mine by the sign in the scarlet prison
Bars cannot conceal!

Mine, here in vision and in veto!
Mine, by the grave's repeal
Titled, confirmed, -- delirious charter!
Mine, while the ages steal!

EMILY DICKINSON

5. NOVEMBER

The world is tired, the year is old,
The fading leaves are glad to die,
The wind goes shivering with cold
Where the brown reeds are dry.

Our love is dying like the grass,
And we who kissed grow coldly kind,
Half glad to see our old love pass
Like leaves along the wind.

SARA TEASDALE

6. WITH A FLOWER

I hide myself within my flower,
That wearing on your breast,
You, unsuspecting, wear me too --
And angels know the rest.

I hide myself within my flower,
That, fading from your vase,
You, unsuspecting, feel for me
Almost a loneliness.

EMILY DICKINSON

7. RISPETTO

Was that his step that sounded on the stair?
Was that his knock I heard upon the door?
I grow so tired I almost cease to care,
And yet I would that he might come once more.

It was the wind I heard, that mocks at me,
The bitter wind that is more cruel than he;
It was the wind that knocked upon the door,
But he will never knock nor enter more.

SARA TEASDALE

8. SHE WENT AS QUIET AS THE DEW

She went as quiet as the dew
From a familiar flower.
Not like the dew did she return
At the accustomed hour!

She dropt as softly as a star
From out my summer's eve;
Less skilful than Leverrier
It's sorer to believe!

EMILY DICKINSON

9. EIGHT O'CLOCK

Supper comes at five o'clock,
At six, the evening star,
My lover comes at eight o'clock
But eight o'clock is far.

How could I bear my pain all day
Unless I watched to see
The clock-hands laboring to bring
Eight o'clock to me.

SARA TEASDALE

10. EXPERIMENT TO ME

Experiment to me
Is every one I meet.
If it contain a kernel?
The figure of a nut

Presents upon a tree,
Equally plausibly;
But meat within is requisite,
To squirrels and to me.

EMILY DICKINSON

11. DEBT

What do I owe to you
Who loved me deep and long?
You never gave my spirit wings
Or gave my heart a song.

But oh, to him I loved,
Who loved me not at all,
I owe the open gate
That led through heaven's wall.

SARA TEASDALE

12. DISENCHANTMENT

It dropped so low in my regard
I heard it hit the ground,
And go to pieces on the stones
At bottom of my mind;

Yet blamed the fate that fractured, less
Than I reviled myself
For entertaining plated wares
Upon my silver shelf.

EMILY DICKINSON

13. WHILE I MAY

Wind and hail and veering rain,
Driven mist that veils the day,
Soul's distress and body's pain,
I would bear you while I may.

I would love you if I might,
For so soon my life will be
Buried in a lasting night,
Even pain denied to me.

SARA TEASDALE

14. I HAD NO TIME TO HATE, BECAUSE

I had no time to hate, because
The grave would hinder me,
And life was not so ample I
Could finish enmity.

Nor had I time to love; but since
Some industry must be,
The little toil of love, I thought,
Was large enough for me.

EMILY DICKINSON

15. COME

Come, when the pale moon like a petal
Floats in the pearly dusk of spring,
Come with arms outstretched to take me,
Come with lips pursed up to cling.

Come, for life is a frail moth flying,
Caught in the web of the years that pass,
And soon we two, so warm and eager,
Will be as the gray stones in the grass.

SARA TEASDALE

16. WITH A FLOWER

When roses cease to bloom, dear,
And violets are done,
When bumble-bees in solemn flight
Have passed beyond the sun,

The hand that paused to gather
Upon this summer's day
Will idle lie, in Auburn, --
Then take my flower, pray!

EMILY DICKINSON

17. THE KISS

I hoped that he would love me,
And he has kissed my mouth,
But I am like a stricken bird
That cannot reach the south.

For though I know he loves me,
To-night my heart is sad;
His kiss was not so wonderful
As all the dreams I had.

SARA TEASDALE

18. LOST JOY

I had a daily bliss
I half indifferent viewed,
Till sudden I perceived it stir, --
It grew as I pursued,

Till when, around a crag,
It wasted from my sight,
Enlarged beyond my utmost scope,
I learned its sweetness right.

EMILY DICKINSON

19. TIDES

Love in my heart was a fresh tide flowing
Where the star-like sea gulls soar;
The sun was keen and the foam was blowing
High on the rocky shore.

But now in the dusk the tide is turning,
Lower the sea gulls soar,
And the waves that rose in resistless yearning
Are broken forevermore.

SARA TEASDALE

20. BEQUEST

You left me, sweet, two legacies, --
A legacy of love
A Heavenly Father would content,
Had He the offer of;

You left me boundaries of pain
Capacious as the sea,
Between eternity and time,
Your consciousness and me.

EMILY DICKINSON

21. A CRY

Oh, there are eyes that he can see,
And hands to make his hands rejoice,
But to my lover I must be
Only a voice.

Oh, there are breasts to bear his head,
And lips whereon his lips can lie,
But I must be till I am dead
Only a cry.

SARA TEASDALE

22. EXCEPT THE HEAVEN HAD COME SO NEAR

Except the heaven had come so near,
So seemed to choose my door,
The distance would not haunt me so;
I had not hoped before.

But just to hear the grace depart
I never thought to see,
Afflicts me with a double loss;
'T is lost, and lost to me.

EMILY DICKINSON

23. UNDERSTANDING

I understood the rest too well,
And all their thoughts have come to be
Clear as grey sea-weed in the swell
Of a sunny shallow sea.

But you I never understood,
Your spirit's secret hides like gold
Sunk in a Spanish galleon
Ages ago in waters cold.

SARA TEASDALE

24. HEART, WE WILL FORGET HIM!

Heart, we will forget him!
You and I, to-night!
You may forget the warmth he gave,
I will forget the light.

When you have done, pray tell me,
That I my thoughts may dim;
Haste! lest while you're lagging,
I may remember him!

EMILY DICKINSON

25. MESSAGE *(also "TO ONE AWAY")*

I heard a cry in the night,
A thousand miles it came,
Sharp as a flash of light,
My name, my name!

It was your voice I heard,
You waked and loved me so,
I send you back this word,
I know, I know!

SARA TEASDALE

26. LOST

I lost a world the other day.
Has anybody found?
You'll know it by the row of stars
Around its forehead bound.

A rich man might not notice it;
Yet to my frugal eye
Of more esteem than ducats.
Oh, find it, sir, for me!

EMILY DICKINSON

27. THE LOOK

Strephon kissed me in the spring,
Robin in the fall,
But Colin only looked at me
And never kissed at all.

Strephon's kiss was lost in jest,
Robin's lost in play,
But the kiss in Colin's eyes
Haunts me night and day.

SARA TEASDALE

28. ALMOST!

Within my reach! - I could have touched!
I might have chanced that way!
Soft sauntered through the village,
Sauntered as soft away!
So unsuspected violets
Within the fields lie low,
Too late for striving fingers
That passed, an hour ago.

EMILY DICKINSON

29. DID YOU NEVER KNOW

Did you never know, long ago, how much you loved me,
That your love would never lessen and never go?
You were young then, proud and fresh-hearted,
You were too young to know.

Fate is a wind, and red leaves fly before it
Far apart, far away in the gusty time of year,
Seldom we meet now, but when I hear you speaking,
I know your secret, my dear, my dear.

SARA TEASDALE

30. I NEVER LOST AS MUCH BUT TWICE

I never lost as much but twice,
And that was in the sod;
Twice have I stood a beggar
Before the door of God!

Angels, twice descending,
Reimbursed my store.
Burglar, banker, father,
I am poor once more!

EMILY DICKINSON

31. LESS THAN THE CLOUD TO THE WIND

Less than the cloud to the wind,
Less than the foam to the sea,
Less than the rose to the storm
Am I to thee.

More than the star to the night,
More than the rain to the lea,
More than heaven to earth
Art thou to me.

SARA TEASDALE

32. THE LOST JEWEL

I held a jewel in my fingers
And went to sleep.
The day was warm, and winds were prosy;
I said: "'T will keep."

I woke and chid my honest fingers, --
The gem was gone;
And now an amethyst remembrance
Is all I own.

EMILY DICKINSON

33. ENOUGH

It is enough for me by day
To walk the same bright earth with him;
Enough that over us by night
The same great roof of stars is dim.

I do not hope to bind the wind
Or set a fetter on the sea,
It is enough to feel his love,
Blow by like music over me.

SARA TEASDALE

34. FORBIDDEN FRUIT (II)

Heaven is what I cannot reach!
The apple on the tree,
Provided it do hopeless hang,
That 'heaven' is, to me.

The color on the cruising cloud,
The interdicted ground
Behind the hill, the house behind, --
There Paradise is found!

EMILY DICKINSON

35. THE GIVER

You bound strong sandals on my feet,
You gave me bread and wine,
And sent me under sun and stars,
For all the world was mine.

Oh, take the sandals off my feet,
You know not what you do;
For all my world is in your arms,
My sun and stars are you.

SARA TEASDALE

36. ANGELS IN THE EARLY MORNING

Angels in the early morning
May be seen the dews among,
Stooping, plucking, smiling, flying:
Do the buds to them belong?

Angels when the sun is hottest
May be seen the sands among,
Stooping, plucking, sighing, flying;
Parched the flowers they bear along.

EMILY DICKINSON

37. WHEN LOVE WAS BORN

When Love was born I think he lay
Right warm on Venus' breast,
And whiles he smiled and whiles would play
And whiles would take his rest.

But always, folded out of sight,
The wings were growing strong
That were to bear him off in flight
Erelong, erelong.

SARA TEASDALE

38. LOST FAITH

To lose one's faith surpasses
The loss of an estate,
Because estates can be
Replenished, -- faith cannot.

Inherited with life,
Belief but once can be;
Annihilate a single clause,
And Being's beggary.

EMILY DICKINSON

39. A PRAYER

Until I lose my soul and lie
Blind to the beauty of the earth,
Deaf though shouting wind goes by,
Dumb in a storm of mirth;

Until my heart is quenched at length
And I have left the land of men,
Oh, let me love with all my strength
Careless if I am loved again.

SARA TEASDALE

40. IS HEAVEN A PHYSICIAN?

Is Heaven a physician?
They say that He can heal;
But medicine posthumous
Is unavailable.

Is Heaven an exchequer?
They speak of what we owe;
But that negotiation
I 'm not a party to.

EMILY DICKINSON

41. VOX CORPORIS

The beast to the beast is calling,
And the soul bends down to wait;
Like the stealthy lord of the jungle,
The white man calls his mate.

The beast to the beast is calling,
They rush through the twilight sweet,
But the soul is a wary hunter,
He will not let them meet.

SARA TEASDALE

42. THE SOUL SHOULD ALWAYS STAND AJAR

The soul should always stand ajar,
That if the heaven inquire,
He will not be obliged to wait,
Or shy of troubling her.

Depart, before the host has slid
The bolt upon the door,
To seek for the accomplished guest, --
Her visitor no more.

EMILY DICKINSON

43. THE PRAYER

My answered prayer came up to me,
And in the silence thus spake he:
"O you who prayed for me to come,
Your greeting is but cold and dumb."

My heart made answer: "You are fair,
But I have prayed too long to care.
Why came you not when all was new,
And I had died for joy of you."

SARA TEASDALE

44. IT WAS TOO LATE FOR MAN

It was too late for man,
But early yet for God;
Creation impotent to help,
But prayer remained our side.

How excellent the heaven,
When earth cannot be had;
How hospitable, then, the face
Of our old neighbor, God!

EMILY DICKINSON

45. DREAMS

I gave my life to another lover,
I gave my love, and all, and all
But over a dream the past will hover,
Out of a dream the past will call.

I tear myself from sleep with a shiver
But on my breast a kiss is hot,
And by my bed the ghostly giver
Is waiting tho' I see him not.

SARA TEASDALE

46. I NEVER SAW A MOOR

I never saw a moor,
I never saw the sea;
Yet know I how the heather looks,
And what a wave must be.

I never spoke with God,
Nor visited in heaven;
Yet certain am I of the spot
As if the chart were given.

EMILY DICKINSON

II

OF MOTHER NATURE

"The lovely flowers embarrass me. They make me regret I am not a bee."

Emily Dickinson

47. THE STORM

I thought of you when I was wakened
By a wind that made me glad and afraid
Of the rushing, pouring sound of the sea
That the great trees made.

One thought in my mind went over and over
While the darkness shook and the leaves were thinned,
I thought it was you who had come to find me,
You were the wind.

SARA TEASDALE

48. STORM

It sounded as if the streets were running,
And then the streets stood still.
Eclipse was all we could see at the window,
And awe was all we could feel.

By and by the boldest stole out of his covert,
To see if time was there.
Nature was in her beryl apron,
Mixing fresher air.

EMILY DICKINSON

49. TWILIGHT

Dreamily over the roofs
The cold spring rain is falling;
Out in the lonely tree
A bird is calling, calling.

Slowly over the earth
The wings of night are falling;
My heart like the bird in the tree
Is calling, calling, calling.

SARA TEASDALE

50. DAWN

When night is almost done,
And sunrise grows so near
That we can touch the spaces,
It 's time to smooth the hair

And get the dimples ready,
And wonder we could care
For that old faded midnight
That frightened but an hour.

EMILY DICKINSON

51. ALCHEMY

I lift my heart as spring lifts up
A yellow daisy to the rain;
My heart will be a lovely cup
Altho' it holds but pain.

For I shall learn from flower and leaf
That color every drop they hold,
To change the lifeless wine of grief
To living gold.

SARA TEASDALE

52. NATURE RARER USES YELLOW

Nature rarer uses yellow
Than another hue;
Saves she all of that for sunsets, --
Prodigal of blue,

Spending scarlet like a woman,
Yellow she affords
Only scantly and selectly,
Like a lover's words.

EMILY DICKINSON

53. WILD ASTERS

In the spring I asked the daisies
If his words were true,
And the clever, clear-eyed daisies
Always knew.

Now the fields are brown and barren,
Bitter autumn blows,
And of all the stupid asters
Not one knows.

SARA TEASDALE

54. AUTUMN

The morns are meeker than they were,
The nuts are getting brown;
The berry's cheek is plumper,
The rose is out of town.

The maple wears a gayer scarf,
The field a scarlet gown.
Lest I should be old-fashioned,
I'll put a trinket on.

EMILY DICKINSON

55. MAY

The wind is tossing the lilacs,
The new leaves laugh in the sun,
And the petals fall on the orchard wall,
But for me the spring is done.

Beneath the apple blossoms
I go a wintry way,
For love that smiled in April
Is false to me in May.

SARA TEASDALE

56. DEATH AND LIFE

Apparently with no surprise
To any happy flower,
The frost beheads it at its play
In accidental power.
The blond assassin passes on,
The sun proceeds unmoved
To measure off another day
For an approving God.

EMILY DICKINSON

57. BUT NOT TO ME

The April night is still and sweet
With flowers on every tree;
Peace comes to them on quiet feet,
But not to me.

My peace is hidden in his breast
Where I shall never be;
Love comes to-night to all the rest,
But not to me.

SARA TEASDALE

58. TO MY QUICK EAR THE LEAVES CONFERRED

To my quick ear the leaves conferred;
The bushes they were bells;
I could not find a privacy
From Nature's sentinels.

In cave if I presumed to hide,
The walls began to tell;
Creation seemed a mighty crack
To make me visible.

EMILY DICKINSON

59. MAY NIGHT

The spring is fresh and fearless
And every leaf is new,
The world is brimmed with moonlight,
The lilac brimmed with dew.

Here in the moving shadows
I catch my breath and sing,
My heart is fresh and fearless
And over-brimmed with spring.

SARA TEASDALE

60. THE BEE IS NOT AFRAID OF ME

The bee is not afraid of me,
I know the butterfly;
The pretty people in the woods
Receive me cordially.

The brooks laugh louder when I come,
The breezes madder play.
Wherefore, mine eyes, thy silver mists?
Wherefore, O summer's day?

EMILY DICKINSON

61. MORNING

I went out on an April morning
All alone, for my heart was high,
I was a child of the shining meadow,
I was a sister of the sky.

There in the windy flood of morning
Longing lifted its weight from me,
Lost as a sob in the midst of cheering,
Swept as a sea-bird out to sea.

SARA TEASDALE

62. POWER

You cannot put a fire out;
A thing that can ignite
Can go, itself, without a fan
Upon the slowest night.

You cannot fold a flood
And put it in a drawer, --
Because the winds would find it out,
And tell your cedar floor.

EMILY DICKINSON

63. THE GARDEN

My heart is a garden tired with autumn,
Heaped with bending asters and dahlias heavy and dark,
In the hazy sunshine, the garden remembers April,
The drench of rains and a snow-drop quick and clear as a spark;

Daffodils blowing in the cold wind of morning,
And golden tulips, goblets holding the rain,
The garden will be hushed with snow, forgotten soon, forgotten,
After the stillness, will spring come again?

SARA TEASDALE

64. IT CAN'T BE SUMMER

It can't be summer, -- that got through;
It 's early yet for spring;
There 's that long town of white to cross
Before the blackbirds sing.

It can't be dying, -- it's too rouge, --
The dead shall go in white.
So sunset shuts my question down
With clasps of chrysolite.

EMILY DICKINSON

65. FEBRUARY TWILIGHT

I stood beside a hill
Smooth with new-laid snow,
A single star looked out
From the cold evening glow.

There was no other creature
That saw what I could see
I stood and watched the evening star
As long as it watched me.

SARA TEASDALE

66. THE MOUNTAIN

The mountain sat upon the plain
In his eternal chair,
His observation omnifold,
His inquest everywhere.

The seasons prayed around his knees,
Like children round a sire:
Grandfather of the days is he,
Of dawn the ancestor.

EMILY DICKINSON

67. APRIL

The roofs are shining from the rain,
The sparrows twitter as they fly,
And with a windy April grace
The little clouds go by.

Yet the back-yards are bare and brown
With only one unchanging tree
I could not be so sure of spring
Save that it sings in me.

SARA TEASDALE

68. BECLOUDED

The sky is low, the clouds are mean,
A travelling flake of snow
Across a barn or through a rut
Debates if it will go.

A narrow wind complains all day
How some one treated him;
Nature, like us, is sometimes caught
Without her diadem.

EMILY DICKINSON

69. THE FAERY FOREST

The faery forest glimmered
Beneath an ivory moon,
The silver grasses shimmered
Against a faery tune.

Beneath the silken silence
The crystal branches slept,
And dreaming thro' the dew-fall
The cold white blossoms wept.

SARA TEASDALE

70. THE SEA OF SUNSET

This is the land the sunset washes,
These are the banks of the Yellow Sea;
Where it rose, or whither it rushes,
These are the western mystery!

Night after night her purple traffic
Strews the landing with opal bales;
Merchantmen poise upon horizons,
Dip, and vanish with fairy sails.

EMILY DICKINSON

71. MOODS

I am the still rain falling,
Too tired for singing mirth,
Oh, be the green fields calling,
Oh, be for me the earth!

I am the brown bird pining
To leave the nest and fly,
Oh, be the fresh cloud shining,
Oh, be for me the sky!

SARA TEASDALE

72. ESSENTIAL OILS ARE WRUNG

Essential oils are wrung:
The attar from the rose
Is not expressed by suns alone,
It is the gift of screws.

The general rose decays;
But this, in lady's drawer,
Makes summer when the lady lies
In ceaseless rosemary.

EMILY DICKINSON

73. CENTRAL PARK AT DUSK

Buildings above the leafless trees
Loom high as castles in a dream,

While one by one the lamps come out
To thread the twilight with a gleam.

There is no sign of leaf or bud,
A hush is over everything.

Silent as women wait for love,
The world is waiting for the spring.

SARA TEASDALE

74. IN LANDS I NEVER SAW - THEY SAY

In lands I never saw, they say,
Immortal Alps look down,
Whose bonnets touch the firmament,
Whose sandals touch the town, --

Meek at whose everlasting feet
A myriad daisies play.
Which, sir, are you, and which am I,
Upon an August day?

EMILY DICKINSON

75. JUNE NIGHT

Oh Earth, you are too dear to-night,
How can I sleep while all around
Floats rainy fragrance and the far
Deep voice of the ocean that talks to the ground?

Oh Earth, you gave me all I have,
I love you, I love you, oh what have I
That I can give you in return
Except my body after I die?

SARA TEASDALE

76. THE OUTLET

My river runs to thee:
Blue sea, wilt welcome me?

My river waits reply.
Oh sea, look graciously!

I'll fetch thee brooks
From spotted nooks, --

Say, sea,
Take me!

EMILY DICKINSON

77. MEADOWLARKS

In the silver light after a storm,
Under dripping boughs of bright new green,
I take the low path to hear the meadowlarks
Alone and high-hearted as if I were a queen.
What have I to fear in life or death
Who have known three things: the kiss in the night,
The white flying joy when a song is born,
And meadowlarks whistling in silver light.

SARA TEASDALE

78. THE HUMMING-BIRD

A route of evanescence
With a revolving wheel;
A resonance of emerald,
A rush of cochineal;
And every blossom on the bush
Adjusts its tumbled head, --
The mail from Tunis, probably,
An easy morning's ride.

EMILY DICKINSON

79. DEEP IN THE NIGHT

Deep in the night the cry of a swallow,
Under the stars he flew,
Keen as pain was his call to follow
Over the world to you.

Love in my heart is a cry forever
Lost as the swallow's flight,
Seeking for you and never, never
Stilled by the stars at night.

SARA TEASDALE

80. LOYALTY

Split the lark and you'll find the music,
Bulb after bulb, in silver rolled,
Scantily dealt to the summer morning,
Saved for your ear when lutes be old.

Loose the flood, you shall find it patent,
Gush after gush, reserved for you;
Scarlet experiment! sceptic Thomas,
Now, do you doubt that your bird was true?

EMILY DICKINSON

81. WATER LILIES

If you have forgotten water lilies floating
On a dark lake among mountains in the afternoon shade,
If you have forgotten their wet, sleepy fragrance,
Then you can return and not be afraid.

But if you remember, then turn away forever
To the plains and the prairies where pools are far apart,
There you will not come at dusk on closing water lilies,
And the shadow of mountains will not fall on your heart.

SARA TEASDALE

82. WITH FLOWERS

South winds jostle them,
Bumblebees come,
Hover, hesitate,
Drink, and are gone.

Butterflies pause
On their passage Cashmere;
I, softly plucking,
Present them here!

EMILY DICKINSON

83. DUSK IN JUNE

Evening, and all the birds
In a chorus of shimmering sound
Are easing their hearts of joy
For miles around.

The air is blue and sweet,
The few first stars are white,
Oh let me like the birds
Sing before night.

SARA TEASDALE

84. REFUGE

The clouds their backs together laid,
The north begun to push,
The forests galloped till they fell,
The lightning skipped like mice;
The thunder crumbled like a stuff --
How good to be safe in tombs,
Where nature's temper cannot reach,
Nor vengeance ever comes!

EMILY DICKINSON

85. IN A CUBAN GARDEN

Hibiscus flowers are cups of fire,
(Love me, my lover, life will not stay)
The bright poinsettia shakes in the wind,
A scarlet leaf is blowing away.
A lizard lifts his head and listens
Kiss me before the noon goes by,
Here in the shade of the ceiba hide me
From the great black vulture circling the sky.

SARA TEASDALE

86. NEW FEET WITHIN MY GARDEN GO

New feet within my garden go,
New fingers stir the sod;
A troubadour upon the elm
Betrays the solitude.

New children play upon the green,
New weary sleep below;
And still the pensive spring returns,
And still the punctual snow!

EMILY DICKINSON

87. LOST THINGS

Oh, I could let the world go by,
Its loud new wonders and its wars,
But how will I give up the sky
When winter dusk is set with stars?

And I could let the cities go,
Their changing customs and their creeds,
But oh, the summer rains that blow
In silver on the jewel-weeds!

SARA TEASDALE

88. FIRE

Ashes denote that fire was;
Respect the grayest pile
For the departed creature's sake
That hovered there awhile.

Fire exists the first in light,
And then consolidates, --
Only the chemist can disclose
Into what carbonates.

EMILY DICKINSON

III

OF LIFE AND EMOTIONS

"I have no riches but my thoughts. Yet these are wealth enough for me."

Sara Teasdale

89. AT SEA

In the pull of the wind I stand, lonely,
On the deck of a ship, rising, falling,
Wild night around me, wild water under me,
Whipped by the storm, screaming and calling.

Earth is hostile and the sea hostile,
Why do I look for a place to rest?
I must fight always and die fighting
With fear an unhealing wound in my breast.

SARA TEASDALE

90. WHETHER MY BARK WENT DOWN AT SEA

Whether my bark went down at sea,
Whether she met with gales,
Whether to isles enchanted
She bent her docile sails;

By what mystic mooring
She is held to-day, --
This is the errand of the eye
Out upon the bay.

EMILY DICKINSON

91. IN A RAILROAD STATION

We stood in the shrill electric light,
Dumb and sick in the whirling din
We who had all of love to say
And a single second to say it in.

"Good-by!" "Good-by!" you turned to go,
I felt the train's slow heavy start,
You thought to see me cry, but oh
My tears were hidden in my heart.

SARA TEASDALE

92. SETTING SAIL

Exultation is the going
Of an inland soul to sea, --
Past the houses, past the headlands,
Into deep eternity!

Bred as we, among the mountains,
Can the sailor understand
The divine intoxication
Of the first league out from land?

EMILY DICKINSON

93. IN THE TRAIN

Fields beneath a quilt of snow
From which the rocks and stubble sleep,
And in the west a shy white star
That shivers as it wakes from deep.

The restless rumble of the train,
The drowsy people in the car,
Steel blue twilight in the world,
And in my heart a timid star.

SARA TEASDALE

94. UNRETURNING

'T was such a little, little boat
That toddled down the bay!
'T was such a gallant, gallant sea
That beckoned it away!

'T was such a greedy, greedy wave
That licked it from the coast;
Nor ever guessed the stately sails
My little craft was lost!

EMILY DICKINSON

95. A MINUET OF MOZART'S

Across the dimly lighted room
The violin drew wefts of sound,
Airily they wove and wound
And glimmered gold against the gloom.

I watched the music turn to light,
But at the pausing of the bow,
The web was broken and the glow
Was drowned within the wave of night.

SARA TEASDALE

96. A BOOK

There is no frigate like a book
To take us lands away,
Nor any coursers like a page
Of prancing poetry.
This traverse may the poorest take
Without oppress of toll;
How frugal is the chariot
That bears a human soul!

EMILY DICKINSON

97. WHAT DO I CARE

What do I care, in the dreams and the languor of spring,
That my songs do not show me at all?
For they are a fragrance, and I am a flint and a fire,
I am an answer, they are only a call.

But what do I care, for love will be over so soon,
Let my heart have its say and my mind stand idly by,
For my mind is proud and strong enough to be silent,
It is my heart that makes my songs, not I.

SARA TEASDALE

98. A BOOK

He ate and drank the precious words,
His spirit grew robust;
He knew no more that he was poor,
Nor that his frame was dust.
He danced along the dingy days,
And this bequest of wings
Was but a book. What liberty
A loosened spirit brings!

EMILY DICKINSON

99. DUSK IN WAR TIME

A half-hour more and you will lean
To gather me close in the old sweet way
But oh, to the woman over the sea
Who will come at the close of day?

A half-hour more and I will hear
The key in the latch and the strong, quick tread
But oh, the woman over the sea
Waiting at dusk for one who is dead!

SARA TEASDALE

100. BLESS GOD, HE WENT AS SOLDIERS

Bless God, he went as soldiers,
His musket on his breast;
Grant, God, he charge the bravest
Of all the martial blest.

Please God, might I behold him
In epauletted white,
I should not fear the foe then,
I should not fear the fight.

EMILY DICKINSON

101. A BOY

Out of the noise of tired people working,
Harried with thoughts of war and lists of dead,
His beauty met me like a fresh wind blowing,
Clean boyish beauty and high-held head.
Eyes that told secrets, lips that would not tell them,
Fearless and shy the young unwearied eyes,
Men die by millions now, because God blunders,
Yet to have made this boy he must be wise.

SARA TEASDALE

102. A MAN

Fate slew him, but he did not drop;
She felled -- he did not fall --
Impaled him on her fiercest stakes --
He neutralized them all.

She stung him, sapped his firm advance,
But, when her worst was done,
And he, unmoved, regarded her,
Acknowledged him a man.

EMILY DICKINSON

103. WISDOM

When I have ceased to break my wings
Against the faultiness of things,
And learned that compromises wait
Behind each hardly opened gate,
When I have looked Life in the eyes,
Grown calm and very coldly wise,
Life will have given me the Truth,
And taken in exchange, my youth.

SARA TEASDALE

104. EXPERIENCE

I stepped from plank to plank
So slow and cautiously;
The stars about my head I felt,
About my feet the sea.

I knew not but the next
Would be my final inch, --
This gave me that precarious gait
Some call experience.

EMILY DICKINSON

105. LET IT BE FORGOTTEN

Let it be forgotten, as a flower is forgotten,
Forgotten as a fire that once was singing gold.
Let it be forgotten forever and ever,
Time is a kind friend, he will make us old.

If anyone asks, say it was forgotten
Long and long ago,
As a flower, as a fire, as a hushed footfall
In a long-forgotten snow.

SARA TEASDALE

106. TIME'S LESSON

Mine enemy is growing old, --
I have at last revenge.
The palate of the hate departs;
If any would avenge, --

Let him be quick, the viand flits,
It is a faded meat.
Anger as soon as fed is dead;
'T is starving makes it fat.

EMILY DICKINSON

107. RICHES

I have no riches but my thoughts,
Yet these are wealth enough for me;
My thoughts of you are golden coins
Stamped in the mint of memory;

And I must spend them all in song,
For thoughts, as well as gold, must be
Left on the hither side of death
To gain their immortality.

SARA TEASDALE

108. REAL RICHES

'T is little I could care for pearls
Who own the ample sea;
Or brooches, when the Emperor
With rubies pelteth me;

Or gold, who am the Prince of Mines;
Or diamonds, when I see
A diadem to fit a dome
Continual crowning me.

EMILY DICKINSON

109. MY HEART IS HEAVY

My heart is heavy with many a song
Like ripe fruit bearing down the tree,
But I can never give you one,
My songs do not belong to me.

Yet in the evening, in the dusk
When moths go to and fro,
In the gray hour if the fruit has fallen,
Take it, no one will know.

SARA TEASDALE

110. THE HEART ASKS PLEASURE FIRST

The heart asks pleasure first,
And then, excuse from pain;
And then, those little anodynes
That deaden suffering;

And then, to go to sleep;
And then, if it should be
The will of its Inquisitor,
The liberty to die.

EMILY DICKINSON

111. PAIN

Waves are the sea's white daughters,
And raindrops the children of rain,
But why for my shimmering body
Have I a mother like Pain?

Night is the mother of stars,
And wind the mother of foam,
The world is brimming with beauty,
But I must stay at home.

SARA TEASDALE

112. THE MYSTERY OF PAIN

Pain has an element of blank;
It cannot recollect
When it began, or if there were
A day when it was not.

It has no future but itself,
Its infinite realms contain
Its past, enlightened to perceive
New periods of pain.

EMILY DICKINSON

113. THE COIN

Into my heart's treasury
I slipped a coin
That time cannot take
Nor a thief purloin,
Oh better than the minting
Of a gold-crowned king
Is the safe-kept memory
Of a lovely thing.

SARA TEASDALE

114. THE PAST

The past is such a curious creature,
To look her in the face
A transport may reward us,
Or a disgrace.

Unarmed if any meet her,
I charge him, fly!
Her rusty ammunition
Might yet reply!

EMILY DICKINSON

115. THE NIGHTS REMEMBER

The days remember and the nights remember
The kingly hours that once you made so great,
Deep in my heart they lie, hidden in their splendor,
Buried like sovereigns in their robes of state.
Let them not wake again, better to lie there,
Wrapped in memories, jeweled and arrayed
Many a ghostly king has waked from death-sleep
And found his crown stolen and his throne decayed.

SARA TEASDALE

116. REMEMBRANCE

Remembrance has a rear and front, --
'T is something like a house;
It has a garret also
For refuse and the mouse,

Besides, the deepest cellar
That ever mason hewed;
Look to it, by its fathoms
Ourselves be not pursued.

EMILY DICKINSON

117. COMPENSATION

I should be glad of loneliness
And hours that go on broken wings,
A thirsty body, a tired heart
And the unchanging ache of things,

If I could make a single song
As lovely and as full of light,
As hushed and brief as a falling star
On a winter night.

SARA TEASDALE

118. I'M NOBODY! WHO ARE YOU?

I'm Nobody!   Who are you?
Are you nobody, too?
Then there's a pair of us -- don't tell!
They 'd banish us, you know.

How dreary to be somebody!
How public, like a frog
To tell your name the livelong day
To an admiring bog!

EMILY DICKINSON

119. MORNING SONG

A diamond of a morning
Waked me an hour too soon;
Dawn had taken in the stars
And left the faint white moon.

O white moon, you are lonely,
It is the same with me,
But we have the world to roam over,
Only the lonely are free.

SARA TEASDALE

120. CONTRAST

A door just opened on a street --
I, lost, was passing by --
An instant's width of warmth disclosed,
And wealth, and company.

The door as sudden shut, and I,
I, lost, was passing by, --
Lost doubly, but by contrast most,
Enlightening misery.

EMILY DICKINSON

121. IT IS NOT A WORD SPOKEN

It is not a word spoken,
Few words are said;
Nor even a look of the eyes
Nor a bend of the head,

But only a hush of the heart
That has too much to keep,
Only memories waking
That sleep so light a sleep.

SARA TEASDALE

122. GOSSIP

The leaves, like women, interchange
Sagacious confidence;
Somewhat of nods, and somewhat of
Portentous inference,

The parties in both cases
Enjoining secrecy, --
Inviolable compact
To notoriety.

EMILY DICKINSON

123. THE DREAMS OF MY HEART

The dreams of my heart and my mind pass,
Nothing stays with me long,
But I have had from a child
The deep solace of song;

If that should ever leave me,
Let me find death and stay
With things whose tunes are played out and forgotten
Like the rain of yesterday.

SARA TEASDALE

124. THE LOST THOUGHT

I felt a clearing in my mind
As if my brain had split;
I tried to match it, seam by seam,
But could not make them fit.

The thought behind I strove to join
Unto the thought before,
But sequence ravelled out of reach
Like balls upon a floor.

EMILY DICKINSON

125. THE WIND

A wind is blowing over my soul,
I hear it cry the whole night through,
Is there no peace for me on earth
Except with you?

Alas, the wind has made me wise,
Over my naked soul it blew,
There is no peace for me on earth
Even with you.

SARA TEASDALE

126. I MANY TIMES THOUGHT PEACE HAD COME

I many times thought peace had come,
When peace was far away;
As wrecked men deem they sight the land
At centre of the sea,

And struggle slacker, but to prove,
As hopelessly as I,
How many the fictitious shores
Before the harbor lie.

EMILY DICKINSON

127. AT MIDNIGHT

Now at last I have come to see what life is,
Nothing is ever ended, everything only begun,
And the brave victories that seem so splendid
Are never really won.

Even love that I built my spirit's house for,
Comes like a brooding and a baffled guest,
And music and men's praise and even laughter
Are not so good as rest.

SARA TEASDALE

128. ASPIRATION

We never know how high we are
Till we are called to rise;
And then, if we are true to plan,
Our statures touch the skies.

The heroism we recite
Would be a daily thing,
Did not ourselves the cubits warp
For fear to be a king.

EMILY DICKINSON

129. THE NET

I made you many and many a song,
Yet never one told all you are,
It was as though a net of words
Were flung to catch a star;

It was as though I curved my hand
And dipped sea-water eagerly,
Only to find it lost the blue
Dark splendor of the sea.

SARA TEASDALE

130. THE DUEL

I took my power in my hand.
And went against the world;
'T was not so much as David had,
But I was twice as bold.

I aimed my pebble, but myself
Was all the one that fell.
Was it Goliath was too large,
Or only I too small?

EMILY DICKINSON

IV

OF DEATH

"Afraid! Of whom am I afraid? Not Death—for who is He?"

Emily Dickinson

131. IF I MUST GO

If I must go to heaven's end
Climbing the ages like a stair,
Be near me and forever bend
With the same eyes above me there;
Time will fly past us like leaves flying,
We shall not heed, for we shall be
Beyond living, beyond dying,
Knowing and known unchangeably.

SARA TEASDALE

132. PARTING

My life closed twice before its close;
It yet remains to see
If Immortality unveil
A third event to me,

So huge, so hopeless to conceive,
As these that twice befell.
Parting is all we know of heaven,
And all we need of hell.

EMILY DICKINSON

133. I SHALL NOT CARE

When I am dead and over me bright April
Shakes out her rain-drenched hair,
Though you should lean above me broken-hearted,
I shall not care.

I shall have peace, as leafy trees are peaceful
When rain bends down the bough,
And I shall be more silent and cold-hearted
Than you are now.

SARA TEASDALE

134. SO PROUD SHE WAS TO DIE

So proud she was to die
It made us all ashamed
That what we cherished, so unknown
To her desire seemed.

So satisfied to go
Where none of us should be,
Immediately, that anguish stooped
Almost to jealousy.

EMILY DICKINSON

135. LONGING

I am not sorry for my soul
That it must go unsatisfied,
For it can live a thousand times,
Eternity is deep and wide.

I am not sorry for my soul,
But oh, my body that must go
Back to a little drift of dust
Without the joy it longed to know.

SARA TEASDALE

136. ASTRA CASTRA

Departed to the judgment,
A mighty afternoon;
Great clouds like ushers leaning,
Creation looking on.

The flesh surrendered, cancelled,
The bodiless begun;
Two worlds, like audiences, disperse
And leave the soul alone.

EMILY DICKINSON

137. A LITTLE WHILE

A little while when I am gone
My life will live in music after me,
As spun foam lifted and borne on
After the wave is lost in the full sea.

A while these nights and days will burn
In song with the bright frailty of foam,
Living in light before they turn
Back to the nothingness that is their home.

SARA TEASDALE

138. I BREATHED ENOUGH TO LEARN THE TRICK

I breathed enough to learn the trick,
And now, removed from air,
I simulate the breath so well,
That one, to be quite sure

The lungs are stirless, must descend
Among the cunning cells,
And touch the pantomime himself.
How cool the bellows feels!

EMILY DICKINSON

139. IN MEMORIAM F.O.S.

You go a long and lovely journey,
For all the stars, like burning dew,
Are luminous and luring footprints
Of souls adventurous as you.

Oh, if you lived on earth elated,
How is it now that you can run
Free of the weight of flesh and faring
Far past the birthplace of the sun?

SARA TEASDALE

140. DEATH IS A DIALOGUE BETWEEN

Death is a dialogue between
The spirit and the dust.
"Dissolve," says Death. The Spirit, "Sir,
I have another trust."

Death doubts it, argues from the ground.
The Spirit turns away,
Just laying off, for evidence,
An overcoat of clay.

EMILY DICKINSON

141. DREAM SONG

I plucked a snow-drop in the spring,
And in my hand too closely pressed;
The warmth had hurt the tender thing,
I grieved to see it withering.
I gave my love a poppy red,
And laid it on her snow-cold breast;
But poppies need a warmer bed,
We wept to find the flower was dead.

SARA TEASDALE

142. REAL

I like a look of agony,
Because I know it's true;
Men do not sham convulsion,
Nor simulate a throe.

The eyes glaze once, and that is death.
Impossible to feign
The beads upon the forehead
By homely anguish strung.

EMILY DICKINSON

143. AFTER DEATH

Now while my lips are living
Their words must stay unsaid,
And will my soul remember
To speak when I am dead?

Yet if my soul remembered
You would not heed it, dear,
For now you must not listen,
And then you could not hear.

SARA TEASDALE

144. I WISH I KNEW THAT WOMAN'S NAME

I wish I knew that woman's name,
So, when she comes this way,
To hold my life, and hold my ears,
For fear I hear her say

She's 'sorry I am dead,' again,
Just when the grave and I
Have sobbed ourselves almost to sleep, --
Our only lullaby.

EMILY DICKINSON

145. AFTER PARTING

Oh, I have sown my love so wide
That he will find it everywhere;
It will awake him in the night,
It will enfold him in the air.

I set my shadow in his sight
And I have winged it with desire,
That it may be a cloud by day,
And in the night a shaft of fire.

SARA TEASDALE

146. VANISHED

She died, -- this was the way she died;
And when her breath was done,
Took up her simple wardrobe
And started for the sun.

Her little figure at the gate
The angels must have spied,
Since I could never find her
Upon the mortal side.

EMILY DICKINSON

147. IF DEATH IS KIND

Perhaps if Death is kind, and there can be returning,
We will come back to earth some fragrant night,
And take these lanes to find the sea, and bending
Breathe the same honeysuckle, low and white.

We will come down at night to these resounding beaches
And the long gentle thunder of the sea,
Here for a single hour in the wide starlight
We shall be happy, for the dead are free.

SARA TEASDALE

148. JOY IN DEATH

If tolling bell I ask the cause.
'A soul has gone to God,'
I'm answered in a lonesome tone;
Is heaven then so sad?

That bells should joyful ring to tell
A soul had gone to heaven,
Would seem to me the proper way
A good news should be given.

EMILY DICKINSON

149. IMMORTAL

So soon my body will have gone
Beyond the sound and sight of men,
And tho' it wakes and suffers now,
Its sleep will be unbroken then;
But oh, my frail immortal soul
That will not sleep forevermore,
A leaf borne onward by the blast,
A wave that never finds the shore.

SARA TEASDALE

150. IMMORTALITY

It is an honorable thought,
And makes one lift one's hat,
As one encountered gentlefolk
Upon a daily street,

That we've immortal place,
Though pyramids decay,
And kingdoms, like the orchard,
Flit russetly away.

EMILY DICKINSON

FINAL THOUGHTS

Thank you for reading my tribute to the work of Emily Dickinson and Sara Teasdale. Were you able to choose a favorite? For me it was impossible!

I hope you enjoyed my selection. It would mean the world to me if you could please take a moment to leave me a short review. Your help in spreading the word is gratefully appreciated, and reviews make a huge difference to helping new readers find our books.

If you wish to stay informed about the upcoming release of new material – plus a chance to win monthly giveaways! - you can enter your email address at www.valeskamatti.com and join our community.

Please also feel free to share any feedback directly with me. You can reach me at valeska@valeskamatti.com. Remember you can also find this book in ebook and Hardcover formats.

Thank you in advance for your feedback! Stay safe.

Valeska

INDEX OF POEMS

II. OF MOTHER NATURE   **51**

III. OF LIFE AND EMOTIONS   97

IV. OF DEATH   143

Made in the USA
Las Vegas, NV
21 June 2024

91322552R00109